DIGGING THROUGH MY ROOTS

George Davson Jr.

authorHOUSE®

AuthorHouse™
1663 Liberty Drive
Bloomington, IN 47403
www.authorhouse.com
Phone: 833-262-8899

Published by AuthorHouse 06/24/2021

ISBN: 978-1-6655-2779-8 (sc)
ISBN: 978-1-6655-2778-1 (e)

Library of Congress Control Number: 2021911257

Print information available on the last page.

Any people depicted in stock imagery provided by Getty Images are models, and such images are being used for illustrative purposes only.
Certain stock imagery © Getty Images.

All sketches in the book were done by the author and artist, George Davson Jr.

This book is printed on acid-free paper.

CONTENTS

PREFACE

I am on a mission to find my roots. I wish to know from where my ancestors originated before they were dropped off on the shores of Guyana. I wish to know their languages, religions, and status in their communities. I know that this piece of history is probably lost forever. In this circumstance, my mission begins with my maternal great-grandparents and my paternal grandparents.

Since *Digging Through My Roots* was first published, several of my relatives have expressed appreciation that they were able to see their place in our ancestral family tree. As a result, they eagerly provided feedback and additional information about some of our family members. I felt the need to share these updates with the family by publishing a second edition. Below are some of the additions and revisions:

- two chapters about life in Guyana in the 1950s
- additional names of relatives and clarification of familial relationships

- additional pictures that expand the gallery of family members
- additional artifacts about activities in the family
- a more meticulous edit of previous information

I would have liked to include research about the life of my ancestors during slavery in Guyana in the nineteenth century, but lack of time and resources have made this a daunting task for me.

Since the first publication, my aunt Agatha, then 100 years old, has passed away at the ripe old age of 103, and so has Shirley Sinclair. On a happier note, Joanna, Bert's daughter, got married and is now the proud mother of a gorgeous baby boy.

I am grateful to all my relatives—Eileen and Lynette Williams and Norma, to name a few—who provided me with information about our past. A special thank you goes out to my sister Pamela, who discovered additional pictures, and to my cousin Yvonne, for helping to solve the mystery of the unique spelling of *Davson*. She shared an explanation provided by Aunt Agatha that the family was originally known as *Davidson* and the spelling evolved over many decades to *Davson*.

Again my appreciation goes out to my wife, Lynette, for assisting me in proofreading and editing the entire manuscript. Her belief in the project pushed me to bring it to its completion. I would also like to thank my friend Handel, an author of several books, for his invaluable guidance through this process.

CHAPTER 1

Ninety-Five First Street

Digging through my roots to understand

the way my branches grew.

—Sallem Haddad

My name is George Davson. I was born on December 14, 1938, in Georgetown, British Guiana, now called Guyana. I am the second child and first son of George and Louise Davson. They named me George after my father, a common practice when naming first sons.

George Jr., 1990

I lived at several places in Georgetown. However, I have the fondest memories of Ninety-five First Street, Alberttown, Georgetown. My family and I spent many happy years there, even though my dad was away serving with the British Allied Forces.

Our house was a beautiful cottage sandwiched between two similar structures. We got along very well with our neighbors. There were three homes on this lot. Our immediate neighbors, the Cambridges (Mr. Cambridge was president of the Transport and Harbor Workers Union), lived behind us, and the Smiths were in front of us.

The Davsons' last house in Guyana

Other families in the neighborhood were the Wilsons, the Sparrocks, the Insanallys, and the Watsons. The area was teeming with children, especially boys. For example, the Insanallys had nine boys and one girl. I guess there were girls around, but at that age, we seldom paid attention to them, or they were so overly protected that our interaction with them was minimal.

As little boys, we engaged in typical male-bonding activities. We went swimming in local canals, and when we felt more daring, we went to the seawall that protected below-sea-level Georgetown from the Atlantic Ocean. It was a treacherous activity, and several young boys drowned in those waters.

One of the most exciting pastimes during the August school vacation was to raid neighbors' fruit trees without the permission of the owners. We played a cat-and-mouse game, especially with the more grouchy owners. Some boys climbed the trees while others served as lookout. We were more interested in the game of avoiding detection by the owners than in getting the fruit.

In those days, parental discipline usually followed the rule of "Spare the rod, spoil the child." Most of the above-mentioned activities happened without the knowledge of our parents. We sought opportunities to escape their tight control when they were away at work, out shopping, or doing other chores. This was not easy, because very few of the mothers went to work.

Some of the families held a tighter grip on their children and provided activities for them at home. I recall visiting the Sparrocks' yard, where we would set up a table and play ping-pong. Of course, their mother was not too far away, and she monitored which of the neighborhood boys could visit. The family lived in an apartment at the corner of Albert and First Streets. It was there, too, that we would meet to select teams to go to the Thomas Lands or our neighborhood schoolyard to play a cricket match or a game of football (soccer).

I have bittersweet memories of playing in these organized sports. My mother was one of the stricter parents in the neighborhood, maybe because of my dad's absence. She had me on a six o'clock evening curfew, which I often broke. Most of the matches went beyond six, and the team would be very upset when I left before the game was over. This would often cause them to lose the game. They eventually started to exclude me from the team, saying, "Davson, we can't pick you.

You always got to go home." I then made the hard decision that I would rather face my mother's flogging, as was the practice in those days, than be excluded by my friends.

Going to the cinema was by far the most popular pastime for young people. I would go to the matinee shows at Empire Cinema in Middle Street or the Plaza on Camp Street. Of all the movies I saw during this period and since, the greatest was the serial *The Drums of Fu Manchu* starring Henry Brandon as Fu Manchu. I can still hear him saying, "I am not afraid of the American, Allan Parker. It is the Englishman, Sir Nayland Smith."

Georgetown was full of eccentric characters roaming the streets. As I look back, some may have had mental health issues. Sonny sold dhalpuri, roti and curry, and potato balls. Barney was a scalper who sold matinee tickets outside the cinema. Another character, Mr. Glasgow, was one who clearly did have mental problems. He would chase after the neighborhood kids trying to hit them with a balata whip because they had called him names. Of course, he was seldom able to catch us, as we bobbed and weaved out of his reach.

Most Guyanese practiced some form of religion

introduced to the country by the colonists. There were Methodists, Anglicans, Catholics, Congregationalists, and Brethren, just to name a few. One of the sects that scared and intrigued me was the Jordanites. They held their meetings on street corners. Dressed from head to toe in white garments, they shared their concept of the gospel to quite large crowds. Most of the people listening were not members, just curious to find out what they were about. Our neighbors the Wilsons were followers of this religion.

My memories of growing up in the forties and fifties in Guyana would not be complete if I did not mention two boys who were not from my neighborhood but with whom I developed a tight bond of friendship that has lasted to this day: Vibert "Hardy" Timmerman and Handel Andrews.

George with Hardy Timmerman

Hardy and I met in primary school, and our friendship developed around our shared love for art. Our most cherished memory was being asked to design and paint the pans for the Kentuckians Steel Band.

I bonded with Handel around academics. We shared a love for language and intellectual pursuits. As we got older, we would visit the law court to witness trials by famous Guyanese defense lawyers like J. O. F. Haynes, Forbes Burnham, and Fred Wills.

George with wife Lynette and children

Joanne and Gregory

I was brought up in a strict middle-class Christian home. My parents had many dreams for the growth and education of their firstborn son. I attended St. Ambrose Anglican and Smith Church Congregational Schools. After completing elementary school, I continued my education at Tutorial High School, founded by the Brothers Castello to provide secondary education for local children. Secondary education in colonial British Guiana was not free, but my parents, understanding the value of education, dedicated their resources to providing us with that opportunity.

After high school, I emigrated to England to pursue higher education. It was the only option for Guyanese students, since at that time, the country had not yet established any college-level institutions. I pursued my college-level education in England and then in the United States. I graduated from Chicago State University with a BA in business and then earned an MA in fine arts from Brooklyn College in New York.

After showing outstanding aptitude and talent for art from my youth, I considered following my inborn gift, but financial considerations led me to take a more traditional path and become a teacher. Little did I know that in this choice of profession, I would be able to explore my lifelong dream of practicing art. I became an art teacher in the New York City public school system, and over the years, I have held many exhibitions of my personal artwork.

I have been married to my wife, Lynette, for over forty-five years, and together we are the proud parents of two delightful children, Gregory and Joanne, and have three beautiful grandchildren. Gregory is a teacher in the New York public school system, and Joanne is a physician in the Orlando area of Florida.

CHAPTER 2

Georgetown, When I Was a Boy

My heart leaps up when I behold.

rainbow in the sky:

So was it when my life began;

So is it now I am a man:

So be it when I grow old

Or let me die!

The Child is father of the man.

—William Wordsworth, "The Rainbow"

Whenever I reminisce about the Georgetown of my youth, William Wordsworth's beautiful words spring to mind. He was speaking about rural England. My reminiscence concerns Georgetown, but nonetheless, our sentiments are the same.

When I was a boy and a young teen, Georgetown was called the Garden City because of its beautiful tree-lined streets and two beautiful landscaped gardens: Promenade and Botanic. Its large poincianas and bougainvillea were fragrant and colorful. Flowers were planted in mini gardens on private property and along the shoulders of streets.

Downtown Carmichael Street

Stabroek Market, also known as "big market," is still one of the most familiar buildings in the city. It is the largest market in the country. Built by the Dutch in 1881 on the bank of the Demerara River, it occupies about 76,000 square feet. It is the busiest area in Georgetown.

Stabroek Market

It was more than a market—it was the commercial center of the city, like the modern American mall. Guyanese came to purchase not only produce but clothing, jewelry, home goods, furniture, medical supplies, and all their everyday necessities. It was and still is a beehive of activity. The scene is replete with donkey carts or drays, delivery trucks, and vans bringing produce to the market from rural areas. At the time of its construction, there was little vehicular traffic, and many farmers brought their produce to the market by boat.

Outside the market was the terminal of the government bus transportation system, bringing shoppers from all over the city and beyond. The bus system has now been replaced by small private vans known as *dollar vans*. When I was a boy, the country had a railway system, part of which carried passengers from New Amsterdam to Carmichael Street (sixty-one miles) and Vreedenhoop to Parika (nineteen miles). It was the first railway system on the South American continent.

As British Guyana developed during the early years of the twentieth century, department stores sprung up to provide more comfortable locations for shopping. Some of these were Bookers Universal, Bettencourt's, J. P. Santos, and Fogarty's, where at Christmas, our mom would take us, primarily in the evening, to enjoy the beautifully decorated windows. We gazed longingly at the toys and other merchandise in the windows, items that many could not afford to purchase.

In addition to the market, there were many other impressive structures around Georgetown built by the British, mirroring the Victorian-style architecture seen in English towns throughout Great Britain. Among these was St. George's Cathedral, rising 143 feet, one of the tallest wooden churches in the world at that time.

Sketch of St. George's Cathedral

Another sight, famous then and still, is the Victoria Law Court, the High Court of Guyana. A statue of Queen Victoria stands in front of the building.

Victoria Law Courts

14

The Carnegie Library, donated by Andrew Carnegie, is another important sight in Georgetown. My first art exhibition as a teenager was on display in this building.

Carnegie Library

The country's Parliament Building is a must-see. It was designed by Joseph Hadfield and built on a foundation of greenheart logs. It was completed in 1834.

Parliament Building

Demerara Ferry between Georgetown and Vreedenhoop

CHAPTER 3

Christmas in the 1950s

No one loves the Christmas holidays like I do, especially the last few days leading up to Christmas Day. The colorful lights around the city, people shopping in the stores and with street vendors, performers at street corners, steel bands belting out popular calypso hits, and seasonal Christmas music—these were the sights and sounds that put me in the mood for the big day.

Decorating the home for Christmas was a big deal. The chairs and tables, rocking chairs, and other wooden furniture were washed and prepped for a new coat of varnish. (In the hustle and bustle of these preparations, some families would get a late start, and the family spent Christmas Day sitting on sticky furniture that had not had enough time to dry properly.) Chairs with tattered cane seats were restrung, and new cushions or throw pillows were added to enhance the decoration. Even the wooden floors were sanded and lacquered to give them a new look.

Sometimes the floors were covered with sheets of brand-new linoleum, so popular in many homes of the fifties. The look was never complete without a new doormat. The final touch was the removal of old window drapes and the hanging of new ones. Many housewives had spent all December fashioning new drapes on their Singer sewing machines.

In a prominent place in the living room was the traditional Christmas tree. Since there were few trees sold in stores, families made their own Christmas trees. Bands of green crepe paper were strung on pieces of wire to simulate branches. The flower vases were full of homemade artificial flowers using similar techniques and were festooned with roses, sunflowers, fern fronds, and dahlias.

The celebration rose to a fever pitch on Christmas Eve. Young women in the family visited friends and relatives to exchange gifts. Young men often had an agenda less specific, roaming around the neighborhood looking for their friends. Moms were at home baking cakes and generally cooking up a storm for the sumptuous Christmas Day meal.

Many dads escaped these domestic rituals to spend time at a friend's home or at a restaurant where the drinks were spirituous and the conversation was highly spirited. Of course, this was not the custom of all Guyanese. Many religious families observed the season by attending a Mass that lasted until midnight.

When Christmas Day arrived, children woke up before the crack of dawn to find some gifts beside their bed, some in stockings, and others under the Christmas tree. They wasted no time unwrapping the gifts to see what Santa had brought them. And so, the fun and games began.

Breakfast was a lavish feast. Pepper-pot, a Guyanese national dish with a rich aroma, was the main course, accompanied by loaves of freshly baked bread. We also enjoyed slices of baked ham and other delicacies.

Not long after breakfast, friends and extended family members would arrive to share in the festivities. We sat down to a sumptuous lunch. The many culinary treats left us completely sated. Additional servings of pepper-pot and garlic pork, a legacy of the Portuguese immigrants to Guyana, were served on plates of cook-up rice prepared in the Guyanese style.

Added highlights were national wines made from rice and jamoon. Ginger beer, mauby, and five-finger drinks were served to the young children in the home. As we pushed away from the table, the gathering splintered off into smaller groups to debate current topics. Cricket and politics were at the top of the list. As the midnight hour approached, the gathering started to dwindle, and sooner or later we all retired to bed thinking about the excitement that awaited us the following day, known as Boxing Day.

Boxing Day was observed as a legal holiday in many parts of the British Commonwealth. It originated with the tradition of giving boxes of food to the poor on the day after Christmas. December 26 remained a legal holiday, even though it had lost its original meaning. In Guyana, it was the day to continue giving gifts to friends and attending as many parties as possible. Parties during the day, known as picnics, were the main form of enjoyment for teens and younger adults. Everyone celebrated the season to the fullest.

Guyanese ushered in the new year in different ways. Some remained at home and lifted glasses of champagne as the clock struck midnight. Some greeted the new year in church, believing it would guarantee them a prosperous year. Still others attended fancy balls where the women dressed elegantly and the men wore tuxedos and bowties. New Year's Day, another legal holiday, gave everyone an opportunity to recuperate from a weeklong celebration. As they savored the memories of the past week, they were already planning for next Christmas.

Kite Flying

"Up from the grave he arose!" The hymn commemorates Christ's resurrection and ascension, and some people feel that kite-flying at Easter is symbolic of this biblical event. Easter Monday, the day after Easter Sunday, is a legal holiday in Guyana. On this day, Guyanese flocked to the seawall to fly their kites.

Young people had spent several days creating their masterpieces, decorating kites with colorful designs and frills of their own choosing. There were kites of different shapes and sizes: boxes, hexagons, diamonds, and even some shaped liked birds. An envied specialty was the "singing engine."

Constructed with an elevated segment resembling a nose, it made a humming sound as it fluttered in the wind.

There was not always a happy ending to the celebration of this annual Easter Monday event. Some flyers attached razors to the tails of their kites. As the kites bobbed about in the wind, their handlers maneuvered them close to other kites and often succeeded in cutting the strings that controlled the kites and sending them spiraling out of control to the ground. So, after all the work, planning, and anticipation of a day of fun, the owners walked away from the seawall or field sad and often in a flood of tears.

The crowds flocked to the seawall because of the beach and the steady breeze of the Atlantic Ocean. The wall, built by the Dutch in the 1880s, is a massive concrete slab extending for several miles along the shoreline to protect the land that lies seven feet below sea level. However, the seawall was not the only place for flyers. The challenge was to find a large open space free from entanglements like trees, lampposts, and electrical wiring. In rural areas, children would tie their kites to a bannister and leave them aloft overnight. They would wake up the next morning to find the kites still dancing in the wind.

Seawall built by Dutch Settlers in Georgetown

CHAPTER 4

Mom

All that I am or ever hope to be, I

owe to my angel Mother.

—Abraham Lincoln

My mother's name was Louise Davson, née Adams. Her parents were part of the new black middle class that emerged following the end of slavery. Her father, a court bailiff, headed one of the well-established families in Georgetown. Her parents did not approve of her marrying a young man from Albouystown, a depressed inner-city neighborhood, despite his decency and career promise. Notwithstanding their fears, he rose to the top of his chosen profession before his retirement. But love conquered all, and the young couple eloped, got married, and started a family of their own.

Mom attended Bishops' High School, then the most prestigious girls' school in the country. Its primary function was to provide education to the children of British expatriates, and this privilege was extended to the children of wealthy and influential local families. Mom did not speak of her contemporaries. However, they must have been the best and brightest of British Guiana society.

Louise Davson with Dolly and baby

George Jr. in arms, 1939

Mom was a housewife who took her job seriously. She was a disciplinarian and used Guyanese adages to inform her parenting. For example, "When you go to crab dance, you must get mud." This means that if you hang out with the wrong crowd, you will get into trouble.

She was up "before the cock crows" in the morning and woke us up to a glass of eggnog. She considered this regimen good for our health and development. She got us dressed and headed us to the seawall. Upon arrival, we splashed in the water, drew figures in the sand, and had a lot of fun playing with other kids.

Mom was a wonderful mother, and no words could do justice to my feelings about her love and care for us. Disinherited by her family for an ill-advised marriage and living in isolation from family support, she feverishly dedicated her life to her new family. She made many sacrifices to enable my siblings and me to be who we are today.

She liked to dance, especially to calypso music. Lord Kitchener, Bill Rogers, Mighty Sparrow, and King Fighter were among her favorites.

CHAPTER 5

Dad

Men like my father cannot die. They are
with me still, real in memory as they were in
the flesh, loving and beloved forever.
—Richard Llewelyn, How Green Was My Valley

Dad (June 18, 1908–June 10, 1983)

My dad was a kind, loving, thoughtful, and respectable person. He was born George Egerton Davson on June 28, 1908, in Albouystown, Georgetown, Guyana. He was one of seven children born to Marian and Jacob Davson.

His earliest driving force was to rise above his humble beginnings. To this end, at a young age, he began a career in the Guyana Postal Service. However, he soon found this to be a rather limited goal.

In addition to this primary job, he became credentialed in business education, excelling in shorthand and typing skill, which he taught in the evenings to students and workers holding key governmental positions. He was also elected secretary of the Guyana Commercial Teachers' Association.

Music played an important part in his life. In his spare time, he taught himself to play the piano and the organ. At one time, he was the assistant organist at St. George's Cathedral.

In 1941, after the outbreak of World War II, he seized the opportunity to travel to England to serve in the Allied forces. The postal workers from Guyana were recruited because of the special skills they had developed in using Morse code to send telegrams throughout Guyana. This skill helped the British transmit coded messages to their allies without detection by the German Forces.

Dad with army buddies

During his tour of duty in the armed forces, he relished his exposure to horizons beyond his narrow life in Guyana. He traveled to other countries and got as far as Aden, Yemen, and the Middle East. My favorite picture is of him dressed in an Arab outfit (a burnoose).

Dad in Arab dress

After the war ended, he returned to Guyana and rejoined the postal service. He continued to work his way diligently up the career ladder of the department. He became postmaster at offices in Georgetown as well as offices in many rural areas. He reached the pinnacle of the organization when he was appointed as superintendent of postal services.

Unlike Mom, Dad spared the rod. He preferred to

discipline his children and keep them on "the straight and narrow" through dialogue. He loved giving long speeches and never lost an opportunity to deliver them. It might be this ability that made him the first secretary of the Guyana Post Office Workers' Union.

Our parents took us to St. George's Anglican Cathedral every Sunday night. They were members of the church. However, during the day, we attended Sunday school at the Salvation Army church because it was a short walk from our home. Back then, it was not unusual to spend several hours in church on Sunday.

When Dad worked at Cornhill Post Office, located downtown close to the Stabroek Market, he would leave me at Humphrey's Barber Shop to get a haircut. I would remain there until he came to pick me up later in the day. The barbershop was located in the second level of a two-story building. On the street level was a large jewelry store.

I really enjoyed this bonding time with my dad. After my haircut, I always asked him to buy me pastries from Brown Betty, a very well-known bakery in Georgetown that sold some of the best-tasting pastries in the city. We would sometimes end the day with a visit to my grandmother in Albouystown. It was there that I became acquainted with the large extended Davson family. There were so many aunts, uncles, and cousins that it took some time for me to get to know them individually.

In 1980, Dad traveled to the United States to join his wife and children who had emigrated earlier. He was looking forward to new experiences in this stage of his life when death interceded.

Dad loved people and was always willing to help less-fortunate family members and friends. To his family, he was a hero. He was deeply adored, especially by his sisters, Agatha and Muriel.

CHAPTER 6

My Siblings

To the outside world, we all grow old but not to brothers
and sisters. We know each other as we always were.
We know each other's hearts. We share private family
jokes. We remember family feuds and secrets, family
griefs and joys. We live outside the touch of time.

—Clara Ortega

My parents had four biological children and one
adopted son. My siblings were Dolly, Molly, and Victor, and
my adopted brother was Peter.

Victor, Dolly, Pamela, and George

Dolly (Yvonne)

Dolly was the firstborn child and, as such, she received special attention from Mom and Dad. Pretty and spirited, she would challenge the parenting skills of this young couple. They doted on her, and their protectiveness increased when she was diagnosed with a bad heart. They were slow to punish her for her little pranks.

I remember an incident when, at about the age of six, Dolly pushed a naphthalene ball into her nostril. Mom immediately stopped what she was doing, scooped her up, and rushed her to the nearby hospital. When the doctor examined her, he reported that there was nothing in Dolly's nose. Of course, my mother, terrified at the prospect of losing her child and angry because her routine was disrupted, had not heard Dolly saying that the ball had fallen out. The two returned home shortly, my mom still fuming but, without a doubt, relieved that her firstborn was safe.

Like many Guyanese young people, Dolly dreamed of leaving Guyana to experience life outside of the limited possibilities in that country. In the early sixties, she migrated to England, where she still lives. In England, she pursued a career in nursing and then in business. She is the only sibling to have followed Dad in developing shorthand and typing skills, which prepared her for the corporate world.

She married and raised three talented children. Her eldest child, Bertrand, professionally known as Jeff Gordon, is a saxophonist who does gigs in England and Europe. Her daughter, Michelle, is an educator and social worker, and her younger son, Richard, is in the printing business. Together, they have provided her with ten grandchildren.

Molly (Pamela)

My second sister was called Molly. Someone thought it was interesting to have two children with rhyming names. It was only at the time of her planning to migrate to the United States that we found out her legal name was Pamela.

Molly is generous and caring and never hesitates to help people in need. She is in many ways the anchor of the family, sponsoring my parents, my brother, and me into the United States. She took care of our mother until her passing. She often must be reminded that she cannot save the whole world. She is, in my eyes, an angel in disguise. Life is full of ups and downs, but talk to my sister, and you will believe that there are only ups. It should come as no surprise that her favorite book is *The Power of Positive Thinking* by Norman Vincent Peale.

Her schooling was at Smith's Church Public School and Tutorial High School. Even though my father tried to push her into a teaching career, she stood her ground and followed a career in nursing. She earned her certificates in nursing and worked as a nurse in Georgetown Hospital before being recruited to work as a registered nurse at King's County Hospital in Brooklyn, New York.

She wore so many hats in her profession, from nurse to supervisor to administrator, that her résumé is as long as her arm. She holds a BA and MA in public health nursing.

My sister loves fine clothes and fine food, and the way she decorates her home is a testimony to her fine tastes. Fine food may not always be good for her health, but I know she is saying, "You only live once."

Her marriage produced two sons. Mark works in a social welfare organization, and Peter is an award-winning film producer, artist, and entrepreneur. The talents in art and music continue to manifest themselves into the second and third generation of the Davson family. Molly has three grandchildren.

Victor

Victor is the youngest of my siblings. His name aptly reflects his birth after my dad's return from a triumphant war. Victor was a welcome addition to our family, but like most young siblings, he often tested our patience. He is ten years younger than I am.

He has the ability to get on people's nerves. He is also a risk-taker. I have two interestingly vivid memories of his challenging behavior. The first is when an Indian boy chased him with a cutlass. Ten-year-old Victor flew like the wind and barely made it through the front door as his attacker stood at the foot of the stairs waving the cutlass. To this day, he has never disclosed what he had done to infuriate the boy.

The second memory concerns his refusal to follow the rules that we all were given. When Mom went to the Stabroek Market to do her shopping, she left us with rules of conduct.

Some of these were not to open the door to anyone we did not know and not to go outside. But as soon as she left the house, the fun and games began. The cookie jar was emptied, and her bed became a trampoline. However, no one dared to go outside except Victor. We only knew he had been outside when he burst through the door yelling, "She coming, she coming!"

Little did he know that Mom had seen him. To our surprise, she only scolded him and did not give him the whooping we, the older siblings, would have received.

Victor was clearly pampered and protected by Mom. She would very seldom discipline him for things he did wrong. We all looked on in amazement and wondered why. Even Dad once said to her, "You're creating a monster you won't be able to control."

Victor has matured into a successful artist and entrepreneur and cofounded Aljira, a center for contemporary art, one of the few black art galleries on the New Jersey art scene. I applaud him because the road to success as an artist is long and hard, especially for black artists. Art is paramount to him, and he has sacrificed much to attain his goals. I am an artist also and have personal knowledge of what I speak.

Victor is now the proud father of two accomplished sons and two brilliant grandchildren. His older son, Egan, is an intelligent technology expert. His son, Alan, has inherited the artistic genes. He is a teacher, an artist, a graphic artist, a tattoo artist, and a budding entrepreneur.

Peter

"What a surprise. I have a new baby brother!" Suddenly one day, Mom brought a baby boy to the house and told us he was going to stay with us and we were going to adopt him. She didn't give us a lot of explanation, and we slowly, one by one, warmed up to the fact that the baby was here to stay. That's how Peter came into our life. What a joyful baby he was! We all took turns taking care of him.

When I left Guyana, Peter was still a toddler, and I got to know him as a young man during my return trips to visit the family. Since we have regained contact, we keep in touch regularly by phone. On several of my trips back to Guyana to visit family and friends, he was at the airport to greet Lynette and me and drive us to where we were planning to stay.

Peter and George Jr.

Despite many offers to join us in the United States, Peter has decided to remain in Guyana and build a life there. He works for the Guyanese government and has held many important positions during his tenure.

He is now the father of a fine young lady named Nathalie. He lives a responsible life and is very active in church. This is Peter, "a brother from another mother."

CHAPTER 7
Grandparents

Nobody can do for little children what
grandparents do. Grandparents sort of sprinkle
stardust over the lives of little children.
—Alex Haley

Maternal grandfather (center), wife, and children

At the outset, I said that I was on a mission to find my roots. My ancestors came from Africa, but unlike Alex Haley's *Roots*, I do not know anything about them. Consequently, my family tree starts with my great-grandparents.

The Adamses

Unlike the Davsons, the Adamses, my maternal great-grandparents, came to the city from New Amsterdam. They were an intact nuclear family, and I have pictures of my great-grandparents, my grandfather's parents, at a ripe old age. My grandparents had four children. Their two sons, Patrick and James, died as teenagers. I got to know and interact with my Aunt Olive, who was still living at home.

My grandmother, Mary, born into the well-known Loncke family, was a warm and caring person. My siblings and I spent many fun-filled weekends at her large property and elegant home in Regent Street. My grandfather, Alexander, who was already deceased, had earned a substantial living working as a court bailiff and had left my grandmother financially independent.

My grandmother's yard had many fruit trees: guava, plums, five-finger, breadnuts, cherries, and downs. She would always get someone to pick some for us. The neighborhood children were a thorn in her flesh because they were always climbing the trees to get some of the fruits.

My grandparents were part of the new black middle class that emerged after the end of slavery. In the afternoon, during our visits, my grandmother would serve us high tea. As we ate, she watched over us and corrected our table manners. They were trying their best to emulate the customs and manners of the colonial masters.

I am lucky to have a legacy of many pictures that give a glimpse of their lifestyle. In each of these pictures, the family is well dressed, the men wearing three-piece suits and the women in beautiful outfits. The family must have been well off to have access to photography in the late nineteenth century. The pictures show the family over three generations. My great-grandfather, born around the 1850s, must have been a child of newly freed slaves. Slavery ended in British Guiana in 1834.

My maternal great grandmother, Antoinette, and her children, Emily, Margaret, and Alexander, 1905

From left to right: My maternal great grandfather,

Adrian and my grandfather, Alexander

From left to right: My maternal grandfather, Alexander and my grandmother, Mary, 1909

Aunt Olive, Mom's sister

**Above: Corinne Sinclair,
Shirley's daughter**

**Below: Shirley Lord-Sinclair,
Mom's second cousin**

The Davsons

My paternal great-grandparents were born in Guyana, but details of their existence are unknown. My grandparents Marian and Jacob Davson were born in the 1870s in Buxton. My father told me that his father, Jacob, was a stevedore, working on the wharves and ports of then–British Guiana. The family seemed to have had a long history of living in different neighborhoods throughout Georgetown: Charlestown and Werkenrust.

Paternal grandmother: Marian Davson

As such, they were artisans, practicing skills needed in urban areas. My grandfather became an entrepreneur and developed a tinsmith business that has carried on to the third and fourth generation of the Davson family.

My grandmother, Marian, was a tall, stately woman I had the good fortune of meeting. My uncle told me that she came to the city from Plaisance. She cared for her eight children for years because my grandfather died at an early age. Without doubt, living in an era when only men worked to support their families, life was difficult for the Davsons.

Muriel and Agatha

Left to right: George, Herbie, and Edgar

Herbie Davson (Joubert)

(March 20, 1920 - April 15, 2004)

My paternal grandmother, Marian Davson

and sons(L to R)Edgar, Herbert, Eric

CHAPTER 8

My Paternal Uncles and Aunts

Uncles and aunts know what made your

mom and dad, but never tell you.

—Anonymous.

My dad had six siblings: Harold, Eric, Edgar, Agatha, Herbert, and Muriel. Agatha, the only surviving sibling, is now one hundred years old. The extended Davson family is huge; each of the siblings has multiple children. I would need an entire book to document the life story of this side of my family. My uncle Eric is said to have fathered more than twenty children.

Harold and Edgar

Agatha (Clarabel), Dad's sister

Despite the harsh beginnings of this family, the children have given good account of their lives. Entrepreneurs at heart, they have all entered the business world—except Dad, whom I have discussed earlier.

Norma, Muriel's daughter

Richard, Muriel, Humphrey, and

Norma, 1998, Alberta, Canada

Norma and her mother, Muriel;

Charmaigne, Norma's daughter

Cousins

Lynette   **John and Pam**

Bridgette   **Johnnie**

Cousins

Hilton   **George (Eric's son)**

Left to right: Norman, Yvonne, Eileen, Lynette;

Faye, Constance and husband Hilton

Finesse

- Floor Scraping

- Refinishing Painting

- Decorating

- Partitions Spraying and Ceilings

For Fine Craftsmanship Call!

Harold Davson

41 Hopkinson Avenue, Brooklyn 33, N. Y.

Glenmore 3-3609

Davson & Davson Tin Smiths

Eric grew a successful tinsmith business and did guttering work throughout Georgetown and beyond. This business has mushroomed throughout the city with his sons, grandsons, and great-grandsons setting up competing businesses. The demand for their services allows them all to earn a living.

Harold, the eldest, was the first to emigrate from Guyana. Starting out as a seaman, he landed in the United States, where he established a construction business.

Edgar was a well-known musician in Guyana. He played the trumpet in the Washboards, one of the local orchestras. He continued this profession in England and was successful enough to have been featured as a trumpeter in a performing band in two movies, *Fire Down Below* and *The Girl Can't Help It*.

Herbert (Herbie), a man of style and good taste, was a mounted police officer before following his fortunes in England. He lived both in England and America before his death.

Like women of their generation, Muriel and Agatha got married and raised large significant families of their own. Agatha had eleven children, and Muriel had six. Together they have countless grandchildren and great-grandchildren spread throughout the United States, Canada, the Caribbean, England, and even Spain. It would take me a second book to trace these familial lines.

CHAPTER 9

The Younger Generation

Gregory, George's Son

Joanne, George's daughter,

and her husband, Rudolph Sterling

Laila and Mason, Egan's Children

Osei, Pierre, Jamillah,

and Sadat

Malachi and Joanne

Maasai, Gregory's

daughter

Kadeem, Michelle, Richard,

Isaac, and Makeda,

Dolly's children and

grandchildren

Zara and Seth

(Joanne's Children),

Dolly, and son Bert

Bert
(professional
name Jeff
Gordon);

Joanna, Bert's daughter

Bert's children: Yannick and Joanna,

(left to right) Nathaniel, Josiah, and Gabrielle

Top row: Mark, Gregory, Egan.

Bottom row: Pierre, Joanne, Alan

Pamela and granddaughter Esabella

CONCLUSION

This book, though limited in scope, has served as a vehicle for recording the history of the Davson and Adams families. The information and relationships I have uncovered enabled me to create a bridge to my ancestors. The interests and talents displayed by current family members were evident in generations before.

My hope is that a member of the next generation will be inspired to seize the baton and run the next lap. It is important to know and document one's history. It is also empowering to know that the legacy inherited can be used as a guide to the future.

APPENDIX I

◆◆◆

Adams Family Tree

James

Alexander

Bella

Margaret

Emily

Alexander Adams and Mary Loncke Adams

(Maternal Grandparents)

Children

James

Patrick

Olive

Louise

George Davson and Louise Adams Davson

(Parents)

Children

George

Dolly (Yvonne)

Pamela (Molly)

Victor

Peter

The direct descendants of Mary and Alexander Adams are very few. Their sons James and Patrick died as teenagers without any children. Olive had a son who died young.

Davson Family Tree

Isaac and Simonette Davson

(*Grandparents*)

Children

Harold Davson

Eric Davson

Edgar Davson

George Davson Sr.

Agatha Williams

Herbert Davson

Muriel Allicock

Children of Harold

Hilton Davson

Children of Eric

May

Joan

Errol

Erickson

Aileen

Rita

Hazel

Megan

George

… and children not listed

Children of Edgar

Edmay

Joan

Jean

Brentnol

Children of George Davson Sr.

Yvonne (Dolly) Gordon

George Davson Jr.

Pamela (Molly) Bonnett

Victor Davson

Children of Agatha

Sheila

Yvonne Lloyd

Eileen

Lynette

Olivia

Raymond

Norman

Warren

Clement

Michael

Children of Herbert

Lynette

Brigette

John

Children of Muriel Allicock

Ernest

Maureen

Humphrey

Rickford

Richard

Norma

Gwendolyn

APPENDIX II

Presentation by George Davson Sr.

Guyana Commercial Teachers' Association

PRESENTS

ITS FOURTH ANNUAL

SEMINAR

AT THE UNDERCROFT, ST. GEORGE'S

on

Wednesday 2nd and Thursday 3rd October 1974

commencing at 8.30 a.m.

Chairman --- --- *ELSIE RODIE (Mrs.)*

Assistant Secretary -------------- *GEORGE DAVSON SR.*

Programme — --- 50c each

PROGRAMME

SECOND DAY

THURSDAY, 3RD OCTOBER 1974

a.m.

13. 8.30 — — — — 10.30 a.m.

Seminar Course—Open to Teachers, Students and Friends

Registration	—	—	$1.00
Course Fee	—	—	$1.00

Note :- After the Course a Certificate will be awarded to each participant.

Winston A. Collins, B C.D. — President, Adjudicator

14. 10.30 — — — — 11.15 a.m

Modern Trend in Pitman   Mr. George Davson
Shorthand   Asst. Secty. (Ac'g)

Introducing Pitman 2000 Shorthand   Winston E. King, F S C.T.

15. 11.15 Luncheon Recess

p.m,

16. 1 00 Pitman Examinations and the new Syllabusses, 1974—75
Mr. I.R. King, Pitman Local Secretary

17. 1.45 to 3.15 Film Show -G.I.S.   1 Typewriting Technique
     2 Kuru Kuru College
     3 Another Film

18. 3.15 Chairman's Remarks

Vote of Thanks   Miss Ruby Whyte

NATIONAL ANTHEM

Prepared by me and delivered in the 4th Seminar of the Guyana Commercial Teachers' Association. See Programme attached.

MODERN TREND IN PITMAN SHORTHAND

CORRELATION OF THEORY AND SPEED FROM THE BEGINNING

Despite the presence of other systems of Shorthand, Pitman's SHORTHAND has survived for many decades. Sir Isaac Pitman gave the world his wonderful method of recording speech by his unique and admirable system of Shorthand. His Centenary Text Book was supplanted by the still popular New Era Edition and of late the trend with respect to Text Books has been added to by the New Course and the Modern Course.

Basically, changes from the Centenary Edition to the New Era have nothing great — simplication of chapters has been the hall-mark of most of the changes.

The trend of the New Course and the Modern Course aims at reducing the time factor of attainment of both the Theoretical and Speedwriting knowledge of the system. And it is interesting to note that apart from methods used by experienced teachers to attain these goals — professional writers of the system have made available wonderful hints; and here I should like to mention some of the rules laid down by a well KNOWN writer:

(1) Penmanship
    (a) Lightness of strokes. Nearly all students write far too heavily.
    (b) Size of Strokes. Students should be trained to write a style which should allow 15 to 20 words to be written in a line of the Shorthand Note Book i.e about 10 to 14 outlines.
    (c) Uniformity of size.
    (d) Technique of writing particular Shorthand Devices.

(2) Encourage fast reading at all times.

(3) Never continue one activity to the point where students are bored with it.

(4) Use rivalry and emulation as spurs to effort. Exhibit good work.

(5) Insist upon neat and orderly work from the start.

(6) The skill, knowledge, energy and enthusiasm of the teaching will foster corresponding qualities in the students.

(7) Make checking a most important part of teaching. The use of records and taperecorders. This is indeed a most outstanding trend which has been a relief to many a classroom.

(7) Make checking a most important part of teaching. The use of records and taperecorders. This is indeed a most outstanding trend which has been a relief to many a classroom.

There is a dearth of **Shorthand Teachers in the field of Speedwriting** (especially highspeed) throughout the world. As a result many classrooms are equipped with taperecorders with extensions to other classrooms and speed practice goes on in the absence of teachers.

DISPELLING THE OBSESSION IDEA OF HIGHSPEED WRITING
(150 W.P.M. and over) as being the real shorthand goal

This trend removes fear and disappointment at one time experienced by students who failed to attain highspeed goals. Today shorthand is taught to be regarded as a hobby acquiring workable speedrates up to 120 W.P.M. as ideal for all Secretarial purposes. Unlike the chase for highspeed rates long ago and the disappointment which many young writers experienced. And whereas in the past the rate of 150 words and over had to be acquired for the purpose of reporting conferences etc. Taperecorders are now used to fill the gap, through Court Reporting and Parliamentary Procedures still call for high speeds from the Senior Staff at least.

APPLICATION OF PSYCHOLOGY

This trend is of invaluable assistance to teachers. A knowledge of psychology is very useful and here again professional writers of the system have come forward with very good ideas. It is plain that:-

(1) The mind should be properly prepared and continuously applied. This is known as the law of readiness.

(2) Making and remaking of stimulous response-bonds. This is the law of use.

(3) Then there is the continuing feeling of satisfaction as a result of the law of readiness and the law of use. This is the law of effect. Teachers must make sure that this psychological trend is working. You must adjust yourself to three important truths. Namely:-

(1) Association is the main cause of the mind's functioning.

(2) Interest decides the course of the mind's functioning.

(3) Attention prevents the mind from useless strain.

UNIVERSALITY OF THE SYSTEM

This trend is unchangeable if not unparalleled. Today Pitman Shorthand is more popular than ever throughout the world. Examination Centres have proved this to be true. More students in Colleges and Schools have found the system rather fascinating in that writing of speed comes in the early stages and note-taking can be enjoyed and a real help to the arduous writing of longhand notes.

PITMANSCRIPT

This very recent presentation of the system as an ideal and beautiful art of speedwriting is moving fast in many colleges and Schools and is accepted by the Pitman Examining Board where certificates are issued.

This, to my mind, is also a step in the right direction. Speed students at examination have no longer to write for a period of 5 minutes, but instead only 3 minutes at a time. This removed the feeling of tiredness at one time experienced by many students at Speed Examinations.

To sum up it can be reasonably assumed that as a whole the modern trend of Pitman Shorthand is to provide ways and means by the acquiring of a quick knowledge of the system of speedwriting along easier and simplified methods of teaching in order to attain workable speedrates and not necessarily highspeed rates of 150 words and over so that for the future we can look forward to perhaps a rapid course Text Book to take the place of the New Course and the Modern Course. This will be, no doubt, the future trend.

Prepared and delivered by George Davson at the Ford Seminar of Guyana Commercial Teacher's Association.

Egan Paul Davson

17 Elm Court, South Orange, NJ 07079

Phone: (973) 763-4940

E-mail: epd3@usa.net

Height: 6'2"   Weight: 170lbs

Eyes: Brown   Hair: Black   Voice: Bass/Baritone

Performance Experience:

Theatre:

Wine in the Wilderness	Bill Jameson	Lehigh University
Dutchman	Clay	Lehigh University
Spunk	Sykes, Joe	Lehigh University
	Slang Talk Man	
Fences	Troy Maxson	Lehigh University
Once on This Island	Tonton	African Globe TheatreWorks

Events:

Cornel West Talkback	Mediator	Lehigh University
Minority Student Awards	Master of Ceremonies	Lehigh University
Banquet '98		

Production Experience:

Who's Afraid of Virginia Wolf	Scenic Carpenter	Lehigh University
The Threepenny Opera	Asst. Stage Manager	Lehigh University
	Scenic Carpenter	
Christmas Follies	Scenic Carpenter	Touchstone Theater
Fences	Scenic Carpenter	Lehigh University
	Asst. Sound Designer	
Godspell	Asst. Sound Designer	Lehigh University

Education:

Lehigh University, Bethlehem, PA

Class of 1998, Bachelor of Arts, Political Science

Courses:

Dramatic Action, African American Theatre

Awards:

William's Prize for Theater Performance, 1997 and 1998

Image Award for Best Actor, 1998

American College Theater Festival Nominee, 1997 and 1998

Special Skills:

Trumpet (Classical & Jazz Band), Writing (Creative & Technical)

Weight Lifting, Basketball, Rapping, Storyteller, Dialects

Trained Literacy Tutor, Chess, Dominoes

Printed in the United States
by Baker & Taylor Publisher Services